Mom, What's in Your Purse?

Seed Learning

Mom, what's in your purse?

A phone.

There's a phone
in my purse.

Mom, what's in your purse?

A mirror.

There's a mirror
in my purse.

Mom, what's in your purse?

A water bottle.

There's a water bottle in my purse.

Mom, what's in your purse?

A wallet.

There's a wallet
in my purse.

Mom, what's in your purse?

A notebook.

There's a notebook
in my purse.

Mom, what's in your purse?

An umbrella.

There's an umbrella in my purse.

Mom, what's in your purse?

A toy.

There's a toy
in my purse.

Let's learn more about Ratha-Yatra.

Color the Jagannath.